EDWARD HOPPER

Painter of Light and Shadow

Susan Goldman Rubin

Abrams Books for Young Readers
New York

Edward Hopper painted scenes of American life. City streets, rooftops, restaurants, movie theaters. But he also loved the country, especially the New England coast, and painted pictures of houses, lighthouses, and sailboats. Sometimes he portrayed places at night, other times in bright daylight. Or when it was half day, half night. He rarely used more than a few people in his paintings, and composed them as though they were part of a theater set or movie frame. When asked why he chose these particular subjects, he said, "I do not exactly know . . . I spend many days usually before I find a subject that I like well enough to do." And when he did, he expressed how he felt about these places through art.

As a boy Edward Hopper loved to draw. His older sister, Marion, remembered that Eddie, as she called him, drew all the time, "even as a tiny lad." When he was seven, in 1890, he received a blackboard for a Christmas present and used it as an easel. Another big Christmas gift, a set of toy soldiers, came from his father, Garret. Garret owned a dry goods store that sold cloth for making clothes, but he preferred reading. At home he had a big library. Edward shared his father's interest in American history, especially the Civil War. He liked to make drawings and watercolors of soldiers. He also produced cutouts that he pasted on top of his paint box as a decoration with the words WOULD-BE ARTIST. Already he knew what he wanted to be when he grew up.

Above:
Eddie and his sister, Marion

Opposite page:
Self-Portrait, 1925–30

Elizabeth Griffiths Smith Hopper,
The Artist's Mother, c. 1915–c. 1916

His mother, Elizabeth, had enjoyed drawing when she was young and encouraged her children to do art projects. She gave them pads of paper, crayons, paints, and beautifully illustrated books. She also took them to the theater. Once, after they had seen a play, Eddie built a small model theater for his sister. Marion put on puppet shows with Eddie as her trusted assistant. But everyone in the family recognized his exceptional talent.

By the time he was ten, his mother had given him "how-to" books and magazines with drawing instructions. For the next year, he practiced with charcoal and white chalk. Like a professional artist, Eddie Hopper began signing and dating his work. Sometimes he copied pictures from books: a sketch of a dog, three birds on a branch, and a portrait of a horse's head. Other times he created original works, such as drawings of a restaurant scene and a row of shops with a grocery store and its delivery wagon. These were very much like paintings he would later create as an adult: *New York Restaurant* and *Early Sunday Morning*. He once said, "In every artist's development the germ of the later work is always found in the earlier."

Starting in childhood, one of Edward's favorite subjects was boats. The Hoppers lived in Nyack, New York, a block away from the Hudson River. In those days the town was a busy port. From their house on top of a hill, Edward could see all kinds of boats traveling on the river. He and his friends liked to go down to the docks and visit the shipyards. They also built model boats and played with them on a nearby pond. Edward learned how to row at a very young age and worked out on the rowing machine in his family's attic.

Then, when he was twelve, he suddenly shot up to six feet in height and kept growing. At school they teased him and called him Grasshopper. Towering above the other boys his age made him feel awkward and different. No longer did he seem to fit in. As a result he spent more hours than ever by himself, reading and drawing.

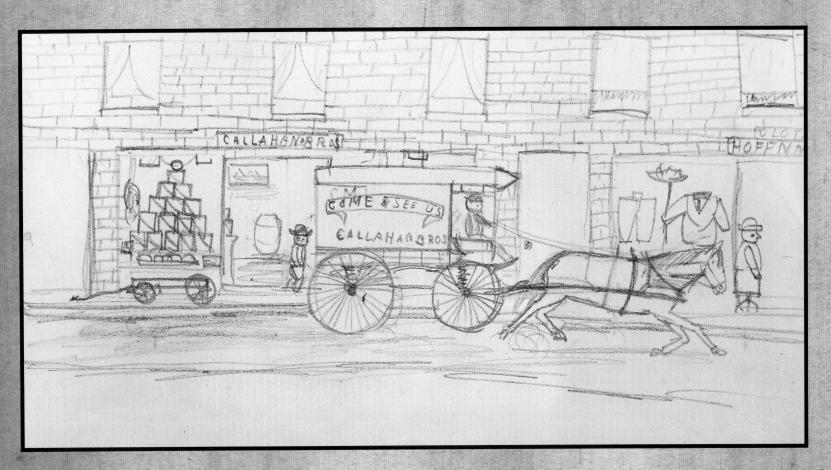

Above: Shops and Delivery Wagon, c. 1892

Left: Garret Henry Hopper,
The Artist's Father, c. 1900

When he was thirteen he did his first pen-and-ink drawing, *The Great Eastern*, inspired by a British steamship. Another ink drawing of a ship included the handprinted words "Alone Alone All, All Alone Alone on a Wide Wide Sea." Perhaps this summed up how he felt. Loneliness turned out to be a recurring theme in his art.

The Catboat, 1922

His father worried about him staying cooped up indoors. He wanted to get Edward out into the fresh air. So he encouraged him to build a cat boat—a type of sailboat with one forward mast and a single large sail. Edward's father supplied wood and tools for the project. When the boat was finished, "it didn't sail very well," remembered Edward. Yet he thought of becoming a naval architect, someone who designs boats. His passion for boats stayed with him. Years later he did an etching, *The Catboat*, featuring a better model than the one he had built when he was fifteen.

Alone, Alone All, All Alone, c. 1898

The words Edward printed on the drawing are from Part IV of the poem "The Rime of the Ancient Mariner," by Samuel Taylor Coleridge. Edward copied this drawing from an illustration by Gustave Doré, a nineteenth-century French artist.

At Nyack High School, Edward had only a few close friends. Ralph Bedell worked out with him on the rowing machine in Edward's attic, and they took turns hitting the punching bag. They also drew together. During this period Edward began a series of self-portraits, thoughtfully studying himself. He hated what he perceived as his full lips and big ears but represented them realistically. He also had a sense of humor. In caricatures he made fun of his tall, skinny body. By this time he had reached his full height of six feet five inches. A cartoon of him bicycling shows his long, thin legs pedaling furiously. Another depicts him taking a friendly beating in the boxing ring from his more muscular pal Wallace Tremper. When Edward graduated from high school in 1899, he did a pen-and-ink drawing titled *Out into the Cold World*. It shows him in a cap and gown, holding his diploma and walking out the door of his parents' house toward distant mountains marked FAME.

Edward knew that he wanted to be an artist and believed in his ability. His parents, however, worried about his future. How would he support himself? They recognized his talent and urged him to go to school and be trained as a commercial artist so that he could earn a living creating pictures for magazines. Reluctantly, Edward agreed.

Edward Hopper Boxing with Wallace Tremper, 1900

Self-Portrait, 1903

In the fall, at age seventeen, Edward began taking classes at the Correspondence School of Illustrating. Every day he commuted from Nyack to New York by ferry and train. The following year he switched to the Chase School, headed by William Merritt Chase, a famous painter. However, Edward learned more from Robert Henri, who soon joined the faculty. "Henri was the most influential teacher I had," recalled Edward. "Henri was a magnetic teacher." He encouraged

The Art Student (Miss Josephine Nivison),
by Robert Henri, 1906

students to express their feelings and personalities. Working with one student at a time, he quietly went around the room critiquing each person's work. If he approved of the painting, he added a red dot. Several of Edward's student paintings have red dots.

Edward also studied life drawing. His illustration courses emphasized sketching realistic figures. A photo shows him working from the model. In those days men and women took life classes in separate studios since women models posed nude and men wore loincloths. Or sometimes they posed wearing costumes. Big sliding doors divided the studios and were opened for school dances and parties. One of the girl students was Josephine Nivison. Henri painted a full-length, life-size portrait of her in her artist's smock. Edward barely knew her then, but many years later she became his wife. At that time his best friends were Guy Pène du Bois, Rockwell Kent, and George Bellows, a uniquely gifted group. Edward sketched portraits of these men, who remained lifelong friends. All of them were to achieve fame as artists.

Although they took art seriously, they liked to fool around and have fun. When the instructors were not in the studio, Edward and the other students boxed with the models, hopped around the room, and ran races while sitting on chairs. At the end of the day, they smeared oil paint scrapings from their palettes onto the walls with their palette knives. And they played pranks on new students. When a newcomer arrived in the men's life class, an older student like Rockwell Kent would pretend to be the teacher, Henri. Then he would furiously criticize the drawing of the best student, Edward. At which point Edward would playfully sock him.

Edward Hopper in Paris, 1907

Everyone recognized Edward's outstanding artistic talent. "[He was] the best man we had at school," recalled Guy Pène du Bois in his diary. Edward received prizes and scholarships and was even asked to teach while still a student. Beginning in autumn 1904, he taught Saturday classes in life drawing and painting. By late May 1905, he was becoming restless and wanted to earn more money than he was from teaching. One of his classmates, Walter Tittle, who was already an illustrator, wrote, "Ed Hopper down at school has decided to try illustrating." Edward worked part-time at an advertising agency and produced cover designs for business magazines. But he didn't like this job.

In the fall of 1906, after seven years at school, he decided to go to Paris and devote himself to painting. By now his parents realized that he was exceptionally talented, and they supported his plan.

From the start Edward adored Paris. In a letter to his parents he wrote, "Paris is a very graceful and beautiful city . . . Every street here is alive with all sorts and condition of people, priests, nuns, students, and always the little soldiers with wide red pants." To his mother he wrote, "I do not believe there is another city on earth so beautiful as Paris nor another people with such an appreciation of the beautiful as the French." He sat in cafés, observing and sketching. His watercolors depict typical Parisians: a workman in a beret, a woman shopping with a basket on her arm.

During Edward's first months in Paris, the weather was cold and rainy and he painted indoors. His dark oil painting *Stairway at 48 rue de Lille, Paris* features the stairway of the house where he lived. It was a Baptist mission. His parents had made arrangements for him to rent a room there through their Baptist church in Nyack. Edward's landlady, Madame Jammes, lived on the top floor with her teenage sons.

In the spring, when the weather got warmer, Edward set up his easel along the Seine. He wrote to his mother, "I am painting out-of-doors all the time now, often taking the boat to St. Cloud or Charenton." These pictures have lighter, brighter tones than those he painted earlier. Later he told an art critic that all of his Paris pictures "were painted on the spot and not touched afterward."

French Woman with Basket, 1906-07

The Rehearsal, by Edgar Degas, c. 1876-77

The architecture of the buildings fascinated him. He said, "The light was different from anything I had known. The shadows were luminous . . . Maybe it's because the clouds were lower there, just over the housetops." The darkness of shadows interested him as much as light as a way to create intense moods.

Edward spent time at the Louvre museum studying the work of the old masters. He also saw many exhibitions of new art. One of his former classmates had moved to Paris and introduced him to the work of Impressionists Pierre-Auguste Renoir, Claude Monet, and Camille Pissarro. The pastel tones of the Impressionists appealed to Edward, and he started painting with a lighter palette like theirs.

The French artist he admired most was Edgar Degas. Degas' subjects—restaurants, theaters, and ordinary people at work—were just what Edward wanted to portray. Degas' compositions excited him. Edward noted the way he composed some paintings on a diagonal, such as *The Rehearsal*, with unusual views, tilted floors, and figures dramatically cut off at the edges. Details of stairs and windows suggest the connection from inside to outside and were important to Edward, too. A few years later, when he painted *New York Pavements*, his composition clearly shows Degas' influence. The scene is designed at an angle and features a chopped-off figure hurrying along past a building with stairs at the entrance and with windows.

New York Pavements, 1924 or 1925

Tugboat with Black Smokestack, 1908

In July, Edward left for Amsterdam, then traveled to Berlin, and finally back to Paris. At last, in autumn 1907, he returned to New York. He had witnessed many artists' work, with different styles and techniques, but was still searching for his true style.

Edward desired a career as an artist. Now, at age twenty-five, he also wanted to live on his own rather than with his parents in Nyack. So he supported himself by doing illustrations for an advertising agency, Sherman and Bryan. He divided his time by working at the agency three or four days a week and painting on his free days and during the summer.

Edward got in touch with his old friends from art school and their teacher, Robert Henri. He showed them his French paintings. Henri didn't like them. "They were too light," he said. Nevertheless, Edward submitted three of them and one of his Parisian watercolors for an exhibition.

Henri encouraged his former students to create a "national art," something more American. Edward tried to

Écluse de la Monnaie, 1909

get away from French subjects and style. Returning to his favorite theme of boats, he painted *Tramp Steamer* and *Tugboat with Black Smokestack*, complete with an American flag flying from the tugboat's deck. These paintings and another titled *Railroad Train* reveal his thoughts of travel and getting away. Edward missed Paris, so he decided to return, saving up enough money for the trip by himself.

In March 1909, when he was twenty-seven, he went back to Paris and stayed at the same boarding house above the Baptist mission. Once again he painted out-of-doors almost every day. Paintings such as *Écluse de la Monnaie*, picturing a bridge across the Seine, show his growing interest in light and shadow, and his ability to depict solid shapes. The slanted blue Mansard roofs, typical of French architecture, intrigued him.

Sailing, c. 1911

A few months later, when the weather turned miserably rainy and he was running out of money, Edward came back to America. He felt he belonged in New York and painted scenes of the city, yet he still liked French subjects and styles. His old school friend and fellow artist, Guy Pène du Bois, wrote, "Something about the French appeals to him . . . He has painted Paris with love in a series of pictures."

So Edward submitted one of his French scenes for a large exhibition that included work by many of his friends—Guy, George Bellows, Rockwell Kent, and their teacher, Henri. But Edward's work was not singled out or sold.

Nevertheless, he stuck to his routine, painting as much as he could and exhibiting his work in various shows. Some of his friends, like Bellows, were getting good reviews from critics. Not Edward. Yet he didn't give up. "I never stopped painting," he said.

In 1911, he did an oil painting called *Sailing*. Working from memory, he created the picture in a studio he was renting on East Fifty-ninth Street. Inspired by his "boyhood boating on the Tappan Zee," his picture featured what he described as a "knockabout sloop rig." Edward had so little money for materials that he had to paint over one of his old portraits instead of buying a new canvas. He exhibited *Sailing* with some of his French paintings without much success. However, he was gaining recognition as a commercial artist.

He was particularly good at drawing realistic figures. *Under Control*, for example, done in gouache (opaque

Under Control, c. 1907–10

watercolor) shows three firemen putting out a blaze. *Boy and Moon*, an illustration probably produced for a fiction magazine, has a quiet mood. The lone figure looking out the window at the nighttime sky echoes a theme that Edward explored in etchings, drawings, and paintings.

Yet he didn't think much of his own ability. "I was a rotten illustrator—or mediocre, anyway," he said. When he made the rounds looking for an assignment with his portfolio tucked under his arm, he would linger outside. "I'd walk around the block a couple of times before I'd go in," he said, "wanting the job for money and at the same time hoping . . . I wouldn't get the lousy thing."

Illustrating stories such as "Home-Sweet-Home" and "Making a Million in Wall Street" didn't interest him. "What I wanted to do, was to paint sunlight on the side of a house," he said. "As a child, I felt that the light on the upper part of a house was different than that on the lower part."

During the summer of 1912, he had enough money to go to Gloucester, Massachusetts, with Leon Kroll, another old friend from art school. It was the first time Edward painted out-of-doors in America, and he fell in love with the New England coast. Both he and Kroll painted realistic scenes. Kroll's work showed crowds of figures; Edward's did not. Boats, buildings, and now lighthouses captured his fancy. Edward said, "Maybe there is such a thing as inspiration. Maybe it's the culmination of a thought process. But it's hard for me to decide what I want to paint. I go for months without finding it sometimes. It comes slowly."

Back in New York he exhibited *Sailing* again. This time a textile manufacturer bought it for $250. It was the first painting Edward ever sold! (And the last for another ten years.) But he kept earning money as an illustrator for advertisements, magazines, and even a college yearbook.

The sale of his painting cheered him on, and he eagerly told his parents the good news. Just a few months later, his father died. Edward felt the loss keenly and was moved to paint a heartfelt New York scene, the *Queensborough Bridge*, in muted tones. Edward saved one of the large unused ledger notebooks that his father had had in his store to record sales. Now Edward noted the date and name of every piece of work he did and the price paid for it, or if it didn't sell, whether it was a magazine illustration or a painting. Just like his father, and perhaps as a way of remembering him, Edward kept neat, careful records.

Feeling more sure of himself as an artist, he moved into a studio at 3 Washington Square North. The old brick building was rundown and had no heat. Edward climbed seventy-four steps to get to his studio on the top floor, and he shared a bathroom down the hall. His high-ceilinged studio had a skylight, which gave him wonderful natural light for painting. One of his neighbors was Walter Tittle, an old friend from art school. Many artists, such as Thomas Eakins, whom Edward greatly admired, had lived at 3 Washington Square. This was to be Edward's home and workplace for the rest of his life.

Edward continued to divide his week between painting and commercial assignments. At that time, 1913, silent movies were becoming a popular form of entertainment. One of Edward's jobs was to illustrate movie posters announcing new films, such as *The Master Criminal*, *The Lunatics*, and *She of the Wolf's Brood*. The part of the job that he liked best was watching the movies. From that time on he loved film as much as theater, and both were to inspire his art. He was to do paintings of the interiors of theaters and dimly lit movie houses. The movies themselves, like glimpses of people through windows, gave him ideas for paintings later on.

Boy and Moon, 1906–07

Night Shadows, 1921

As he tried to achieve his own style as a painter, he experimented with a different medium: etching. He bought a printing press for his studio and taught himself how to make prints. At the Metropolitan Museum of Art, he studied the etchings of Rembrandt van Rijn and Francisco de Goya. When he did his own prints, he began by drawing on paper. Then he repeated the outline of the composition on a metal plate, which was then used to produce multiple prints. For the actual printing, Edward used the whitest paper he could find and the "most intense black ink," which he sent for from London. He drew from memory, recalling places and people he had observed. *American Landscape*, a country scene, shows cows crossing a deserted railroad track with a single house looming in the distance. A grander old-fashioned house with a wraparound porch is featured in *House on a Hill (The Buggy)*. But his etching *Night Shadows* portrays an eerie city street, with a man walking toward a shadow cast by a streetlight. In his etchings Edward explored contrasting themes of city and country, and night and day, that he would later develop in his paintings. When he exhibited his prints in New York galleries and at the Chicago Society of Etchers, he finally had success. People liked his etchings and snapped them up. The printing press remained a permanent fixture of his studio, and he once drew a tender portrait of it with his hat hanging on the edge.

His patriotic posters brought him fame and money, too. In 1917, when the United States entered World War I, Edward tried to enlist. But at age thirty-five he was too old. When the age was extended to forty-five the following year, he tried again. This time he was turned down because he was the only son of a widowed mother. So, instead of joining

Hopper's hat on his etching press, undated

the army or navy, he inspired other men to enlist through the posters he created. In 1918 he entered a contest sponsored by the United States Shipping Board Emergency Fleet Corporation. The agency had been formed to build, buy, and rent vessels needed for the war effort. Edward visited the shipyard to get the feel of the place. "I got this big Irishman to pose for me," he said. The result was a poster titled *Smash the Hun* (a German soldier in World War I) that won first prize: three hundred dollars! Edward did other posters for the American Red Cross that were displayed along Fifth Avenue in New York City to raise funds.

During the summer of 1919, he had earned enough from the sale of his posters and prints to go to Monhegan, Maine, with his art school pals Guy Pène du Bois and C. K. Chatterton. It was like old times as they sketched portraits of each other and painted outdoors. Edward had first visited Monhegan by himself in the summers of 1916 and 1917, and he liked the island so much that he kept returning. Over and over he painted slightly different views of *Blackhead, Monhegan*, studying the way the light hit the rocky cliffs above the sea.

Guy cared deeply about Edward's artistic goal. How could he help him? "In those days," Edward later recalled, "the young artist didn't have much of a chance. There weren't . . . many galleries . . . and very few could take the work of a young artist."

Guy had an idea. He had had a one-man show at a new gallery, the Whitney Studio Club, founded by Gertrude Vanderbilt Whitney, a rich sculptor. They had become friends,

Jo Painting, 1936

Blackhead, Monhegan, 1916–19

and he talked her into giving Edward a chance. In January 1920, Edward opened his first one-man show at the Whitney Club. The paintings he chose for the exhibit were mostly the ones he had done in France and a few from Maine. None of the paintings sold. All were marked "Returned" in his notebook/ledger.

However, there was a greater demand for his etchings, and those sold well. So that summer he could afford to return to New England to paint. At a boardinghouse in Ogunquit, Maine, he bumped into Josephine Nivison, nicknamed Jo. She had been his classmate at art school and remembered him. Jo had also continued painting and exhibiting whenever she could. She supported herself by teaching children at a

The Mansard Roof, 1923

New York school and lived on Ninth Street in Greenwich Village, not far from Edward's studio on Washington Square. Like him, she loved going to New England to paint. In the summer of 1923, they met again in Gloucester, Massachusetts, a charming seacoast town.

This time Edward paid greater attention to her. Jo traveled with her "adored pussy cat Arthur," a stray alley cat she had found on Ninth Street.

The first thing Edward said to her in Gloucester was, "Hey, I saw your cat yesterday." They sat on a fence, and Edward drew a map of the town for her. Each day they went out together to paint. Jo worked in watercolors and gave Edward the idea of using that medium, too. He concentrated on houses as well as views of the harbor. "At Gloucester, when everyone else would be painting ships and the waterfront," he recalled, "I'd just go around looking at houses." He particularly liked the area "where the old sea captains had their houses. It interested me," he said, "because of the variety of roofs and windows, the Mansard roof which has always interested me." He sat out on the street and painted *The Mansard Roof* with its architectural details—porches shaded by awnings, dormer windows, and chimneys. Meanwhile, Jo chose entirely different subjects: churches, children, flowers, and, of course, Arthur.

Chop Suey, 1929

She and Edward were total opposites. Jo was short, barely five feet one inch, and weighed only one hundred pounds. He, at six feet five, towered over her. She was talkative and outgoing; he was quiet and shy. Even in their painting she worked from "a worm's eye view," while he had a "bird's eye view." But they both loved art and French poetry. That summer in Gloucester, their friendship blossomed into a romance. One day they went to see a puppet show based on the folk song "Frog Went a-Courtin'." The puppets, a "long & gangly frog" wooing a female mouse, seemed just like them.

Back in New York they saw more and more of each other. Often they ate at a Chinese restaurant that Edward later portrayed in a painting, *Chop Suey*. He sent Jo French poems and drew a romantic Christmas card for her.

Together they lugged their artwork around town, trying to interest curators and dealers. When the Brooklyn Museum invited Jo to show some of her watercolors, she suggested that they consider Edward's, too. As a result the museum exhibited six of his Gloucester watercolors. Art critics raved about his work. But they ignored Jo's. The

Brooklyn Museum bought his painting *The Mansard Roof* for one hundred dollars. This was the second painting he had ever sold!

When the next summer rolled around, Edward and Jo argued about where they'd go to paint. He wanted to return to Gloucester. She preferred joining old friends in an artists' colony on Cape Cod. They settled the disagreement by getting married that very day, July 9, 1924, and going to Gloucester. It was just before Edward's forty-second birthday. Jo was forty-one. For their honeymoon they stayed at the same boardinghouse where they had stayed the previous summer, and they painted.

Jo Sketching at Good Harbor Beach, 1923-24

Victorian House, 1923 or 1924

From then on Jo became Edward's only female model. Not only did he do portraits of her, but she posed for almost every drawing and painting he did that included a woman's figure. Although she often asked him to pose for her, he rarely did. From the time of their marriage, his painting career came first over hers.

Back in New York, Jo moved into Edward's studio.

With Arthur. Edward felt jealous of the cat. He drew a cartoon titled *The Great God Arthur* (with a caption reading, "Status Quo"). It shows Jo and a human-size Arthur sitting at the table enjoying dinner while skinny little Edward crawls on the floor, begging for scraps. Jo hated cooking. It took too much valuable time away from painting, she felt, so she prepared meals by heating cans of soup and beans. Or they ate out at diners and cheap restaurants. The kitchenette in the studio was tiny. They had to haul coal up seventy-four steps to fuel the potbellied stove, their only source of heat, which they affectionately called "Mademoiselle." But they both chose to live a simple, thrifty life in order to devote themselves to art.

Edward still didn't have a gallery to show his work. One day in the fall of 1924, he gathered up his courage and took his watercolors to the gallery that represented his friend Guy. That dealer turned him down. As Edward passed the Rehn Gallery on Fifth Avenue, which represented his other friend George Bellows, he stopped in. The owner, Frank K. M. Rehn, said that he didn't have time to see Edward. He told him to leave his paintings in the back room and he'd look at them after lunch. At that moment a customer came in and gazed at Edward's painting of a Victorian house. "Just like my grandmother's," he said with pleasure. Rehn immediately sold him the painting and became Edward's gallery dealer for life!

That fall Rehn held an exhibit of Edward's New England watercolors and sold all sixteen pieces. He was very excited about his new artist. The demand for Edward's work far exceeded the supply. Prominent people in the art world, such as a trustee of the Museum of Fine Arts in Boston, purchased his work. Even his friend George Bellows bought *Italian Quarter*, one of his Gloucester watercolors. At last Edward could afford to give up his commercial art! He even stopped making etchings. Instead, he built a huge easel and focused on painting in oils.

Boldly, he experimented with new subjects and portrayed views of America that had never been done before. The 1920s marked a period of art called the Machine Age. Painters such as Charles Sheeler and Georgia O'Keeffe

Radiator Building—Night, New York, by Georgia O'Keeffe, 1927

Room in Brooklyn, 1932

celebrated industry and architecture in their art. O'Keeffe, for instance, created many dramatic paintings of New York skyscrapers and the New York skyline. Edward chose a totally different viewpoint and mood. *New York Pavements* (see page 13) shows a nursemaid pushing a baby carriage out on the city street past the curtained windows of an apartment building. The composition shows the scene from above on a diagonal, which creates a sense of action. *Room in Brooklyn*, however, shows a woman *inside* an apartment. She sits quietly in a chair, her back to the viewer, and faces a window that looks *out* onto rooftops across the way. In other paintings, the viewer and Edward are on the *outside* looking *into* a window. *Apartment Houses* depicts a woman, perhaps a maid, wearing an apron and making a bed. The bright white of the windowsill and the patch of light on the floor indicate that it's daytime. *Room in New York*, however, is a nighttime scene. A man and a woman sit in the same room but seem totally disconnected. He reads the paper while she plays a note on a piano. Are they bored, or did they have a fight? When asked about this painting, Edward said, "The idea had been in my mind a long time before I painted it. It was suggested by glimpses of lighted interiors seen as I walked along the city streets at night, probably near the district where I live (Washington Square), although it's no particular street or house, but it is rather a synthesis of many impressions." Edward's dark night scenes express a sense of secrecy, and perhaps tell about feelings hidden during the day.

These paintings brought Edward recognition and success. He exhibited *Room in New York* at the new Whitney Museum and entered *Apartment Houses* in a show at the Pennsylvania Academy of Art. The academy purchased the painting, and he was thrilled.

Apartment Houses, 1923

Room in New York, 1932

House by the Railroad, 1925

In other paintings he portrayed scenes from the country and seacoast. He did *House by the Railroad* from memory. Critics thought they could identify the house in Nyack that was the model for the painting. However, Jo said, "He did it out of his head. He has seen so many of them." This house, too, features the sloped Mansard roof that Edward had admired in French architecture. But there's a spooky, eerie mood about the house. It looks deserted, yet some of the window shades are pulled up as if someone may be inside.

Critics loved the painting when Edward showed it in an exhibition. So did art lovers. A new patron, Stephen Clark, heir to the Singer sewing machine fortune and a client of the Rehn Gallery, bought *House by the Railroad*. Later, in January 1930, he gave it as a gift to the Museum of Modern

Art in New York. The museum had just opened in November 1929 and had acquired photographs, prints, and drawings. *House by the Railroad* was the first painting by any artist to become part of the museum's permanent collection. When filmmaker Alfred Hitchcock later saw it, he based the weird house in his horror movie *Psycho* on the one in Edward's painting.

Edward's city scenes often depict a solitary person. *Automat*, for instance, features a woman sitting by herself at a table, lost in her thoughts. As usual, Jo posed for the painting. "She always posed for everything," said Edward. Jo even bought the props for paintings, gave them titles, and wrote about them in her own notebook.

She was the model for both women in *Two on the Aisle*, a picture that captures the moment at the theater when the audience is just arriving. Edward and Jo both loved seeing plays and movies. Spending money on tickets was one of their few luxuries. When he was stuck for an idea for a painting, he would go to the movies day after day. *New York Movie* began with a crayon sketch at the Palace Theater. After fifty more sketches, he was ready to paint. Jo posed for the women moviegoers and the usherette. She stood in the cold hallway outside their studio/apartment and held a flashlight. In those days movie theaters had ushers in uniforms who carried flashlights to help escort patrons to their seats. The usherette in Edward's painting doesn't seem interested in the movie being shown on the left side of the canvas. Instead, she looks downward, her chin cupped in her hand, absorbed in her own thoughts. Does the movie bore her because she has seen it so many times? Or is something troubling her?

New York Movie, 1939

Far left: Palace: Study for
New York Movie, 1939

Left: Study for New York Movie,

1939

Region of Brooklyn Bridge Fantasy, by John Marin, 1932

Art critics commented that loneliness was a main theme of Edward's art. However, Edward said that although the mood of loneliness might be in his paintings, he didn't intend it. "The emphasis on it annoyed him," wrote Lloyd Goodrich, director of the Whitney Museum, who knew him well. He quoted Edward as saying, "The loneliness thing is overdone."

Edward's fame kept growing. Goodrich, also editor of *The Arts* magazine, wrote, "It is hard to think of another painter who is getting more of the quality of America into his canvases than Edward Hopper." However, other reviewers thought Edward's art was too literal and academic, even old-fashioned. They preferred the paintings of "the brilliant modernists" who were exploring Cubism, such as John Marin and Joseph Stella. Marin depicted New York skyscrapers as explosive forms, masses of piled-up buildings.

Nevertheless Edward's painting *Two on the Aisle*

brought the highest price paid up to then for one of his works: fifteen hundred dollars! He and Jo splurged by purchasing their first car, a used Dodge. Now they were able to take off and drive in search of subjects to paint.

In the summer of 1927, they drove to Maine. Edward felt inspired to paint *Lighthouse Hill* in oil. He also worked in watercolor. Lighthouses fascinated him. He liked the stark vertical shapes. Critics commented that the lighthouses were really self-portraits, tall and spare like Edward. When he and Jo went back to Cape Elizabeth, Maine, he painted *The Lighthouse at Two Lights*. Immediately, he sold the painting to friends who were collectors.

The Lighthouse at Two Lights, 1929

Jo in Wyoming, 1946

Sometimes Edward and Jo drove west across America. They enjoyed visiting New Mexico, Utah, and California. If they saw a scene they wanted to paint, they stopped. "He sat in the back seat," wrote Jo in her diary, "cursing constantly at smaller space in this car . . . I in the front seat had the wheel in my way & nothing to prop up my watercolor paper—but we managed somehow."

Two painters living together proved difficult. Edward's career overshadowed hers, and Jo resented it. When her pictures were rejected by museums for exhibition, she joked that Edward was "her tallest handicap." Yet she supported his work and felt proud to be married to a great artist.

In 1929, many Americans were hit hard by the Great Depression and struggled to earn a living. The stock market had crashed. Banks, factories, and businesses closed. People lost their jobs and homes. Yet Edward kept exhibiting and selling his work. The Museum of Modern Art included him in a group show, "Paintings by Nineteen Living Americans." The following winter the Whitney Museum of American Art bought a painting he had just finished, *Early Sunday Morning*. Originally called *Seventh Avenue Shops*, the cityscape shows a row of two-story buildings beneath a band of bright blue sky. "It wasn't necessarily Sunday," he said. "That word was tacked on later by someone else." But the empty New York street without figures suggests a time and day of the week when people are not out and about.

Edward and Jo divided their time between the city and the country. In the summer of 1930, they went up to Provincetown on Cape Cod, Massachusetts. They particularly liked Truro, a little town just below the cape, and they rented a cottage on a farm there. "We like it very much here at South Truro," Edward wrote to his friend and fellow artist, C. K. Chatterton. "Fine big hills of sand, a desert on a small scale with fine dune formations, a very open almost treeless country—I think you would like it. I have one canvas and am starting another."

Early Sunday Morning, 1930

Hills, South Truro, 1930

Hills, South Truro shows the dunes stretching out to the sea beyond, and the railroad tracks cutting across the landscape. Edward wrote to his friend Guy Pène du Bois that the oil "was done almost entirely on the spot" when "the mosquitoes were terrible." Jo described the painting as "a canvas that he's grouching over—rather a beauty—hills & hills on over to the sea that he's working on from 6 to 8PM."

When Edward did a painting out-of-doors, he worked the same hours every day so that the light would be consistent.

Somehow they managed to take time off to go to the beach and swim in the bay. Together they did the chores. Jo pumped water to wash the clothes and sheets, and he wrung them out and hung them up to dry. "Things looked so white blowing in the wind," she wrote to a friend, "we got quite excited over it . . . This is the first time we've ever had a little house all to ourselves & we're having great joy of it."

However, one summer when they returned, it rained so hard they named their house "Bird Cage Cottage." Rain splashed in from all sides, and there was no room for Edward to paint indoors during bad weather. But he was able to write letters. That rainy summer Edward busily corresponded with the director of the Museum of Modern Art. The museum planned to give Edward a retrospective exhibition in the fall. It was Edward's first retrospective and a great honor for him. The exhibit opened in November 1933 and included his oil paintings, such as *Lighthouse at Two Lights*, watercolors, prints, and sketches of Parisians he had done as a young man. "Beautiful exhibition beautifully presented," wrote a critic in *The New York Times*, praising Edward as "one of America's most vital, original, and accomplished artists."

The following spring Edward turned to a different project. He and Jo had bought a piece of land in Truro and decided to build their own house. Edward designed it. By July construction was finished and they moved in. It was a simple house with a large, high-ceilinged studio, an enormous window with thirty-six panes of glass, a small bedroom, a kitchen, and a bathroom. The studio and bedroom faced the sea, which gave Edward a wonderful feeling of being on a ship. The view reminded him of the view of the Hudson River from his parents' house in Nyack. He could hardly wait to bring his mother to the house and show it to her.

Edward Hopper in front of his house
in South Truro, Mass., with
Josephine Hopper in the distance,
August 1960

House at Dusk, 1935

At age eighty-one she was frail and confined to a wheelchair, so the visit was postponed. Edward realized that she was nearing the end of her life. In *House at Dusk* he expressed his feelings about her. The oil shows the top floor of a New York apartment building at twilight. The woods behind the building are already dark. For Edward sunlight represented life. He often quoted a poem about evening by Johann Wolfgang von Goethe that he knew in German and English. The closing lines went:

All the birds are quiet in the woods
Soon you will rest too.

He delivered the painting to the Rehn Gallery in January 1935, and his mother died a couple of months later. Deeply saddened, Edward lost interest in painting for a while.

Ground Swell, 1939

emotions without picturing people and places. Jackson Pollock, a leader of the style, didn't use a traditional easel or oil paint and watercolor. Instead, he spread his canvas on the floor and poured and dripped household paint directly from the cans, swirling the paint with a stick.

Edward, however, continued on his own course of realism even though many artists at that time were turning to abstract painting. Despite his years of experience and success, painting didn't come any easier. "Art is like life itself," said Edward, "it's a lot of hard work." Sometimes he only did two or three oil paintings a year.

Then, the next summer at Truro, he felt cheered by his surroundings and produced many paintings of sailboats. Jo watched *Ground Swell* in progress and wrote, "It ought to be [a] beauty." Shades of blue and white capture the excitement of the young men sailing. The viewer can almost feel the wind blowing and smell the salt air. Edward still longed to go sailing the way he had as a boy, but Jo wouldn't let him. She said, "He's too good a man to lose that way."

Now they routinely spent half the year in Truro and the other half in New York. Edward's work brought him more and more fame, prizes, and honors. His art was praised for its honesty and poetry. A critic in *Time* magazine hailed Edward as "a painter of the American scene." But critic Clement Greenberg disagreed and called Hopper a "bad painter." He wrote, "Hopper's painting is essentially photography, and it is literary in the way that the best photography is." Greenberg championed the new movement called Abstract Expressionism, which was painting that expressed artists'

Composition with Pouring II,
by Jackson Pollock, 1966

Cape Cod Evening, 1939

In July 1939, he was trying to find a subject that he wanted to paint. Nothing interested him in Truro, so he drove to a nearby town, Orleans, and saw a location he thought he could use. On the spot he made sketches of a doorway, then a grove of locust trees nearby. Back in his studio he began to compose the painting with sketches done from life and "mental impressions of the vicinity." The picture shows a man, a woman, and a dog: together, yet separate. "The figures were done almost entirely without models," Edward said, "and the dry, blowing grass can be seen from my studio window in late summer or autumn . . . the dog is listening to something, probably a whippoorwill or some evening sound."

Edward made the dog a collie. As he worked on the painting, he needed to check some physical details about the breed and went to the Truro Library. He looked in an encyclopedia and discovered there were no collies pictured.

Gas, 1940

Yet he wanted his painting to be realistic. When he and Jo parked the car near a store, "there was this small miracle," remembered a friend and fellow printmaker. "Just the type of dog that was wanted [a collie] came out of the car ahead—with a child while the mother went in the nearby store to shop. Jo made friends with the children and dog—Edward got out his sketch book and pencil and while Jo held the dog with patting . . . Edward got his sketch." Jo helped Edward give the painting its name. At first they thought of *The Whippoorwill* and *After Supper*, but finally they decided on *Cape Cod Evening*.

One of his next paintings features a subject that had never been done before in fine art: a gas station, a very ordinary subject. Edward had had the idea for years. Jo wrote to his sister, Marion, about it and said that what he wanted to achieve was "an effect of night on a gasoline station . . . at twilight, with the lights over the pumps lit." Edward couldn't find any real station that was exactly what he had in mind, so he made sketches of various places. "When we go to look at them," Jo wrote, "around here they aren't lit at all. They're not wasting Elec. [electricity] till it's pitch dark, later than Ed wants. He's painting in the studio entirely now."

Self-Portrait, by Josephine N. Hopper

A few days later, Jo gave Marion another progress report. "Ed's canvas is coming on nicely. The pumps are shining red—and the lights above so bright and the trees dark beyond and a road going off in the distance." Edward even added a Mobil gas sign. The winged horse seems to magically fly off to the woods. One of the places he had sketched was the Mobil gas station in Truro. Later he gave an autographed reproduction of the painting to the owner of the station, who treasured it. Edward finished the picture and called it *Gas*. The painting seems to express his concern about the city encroaching on the country, people and cars spoiling the natural beauty of the American landscape.

When things went slowly and he couldn't come up with an idea, he spent more time than ever reading. One of his favorite poets was Robert Frost, and Jo did a portrait, *Edward Hopper Reading Robert Frost*. It shows Edward sitting in a cozy spot near the potbellied stove in Truro, deeply absorbed in his book. At last he posed for her!

A short story, "The Killers," by Ernest Hemingway, partly inspired one of his best-known paintings, *Nighthawks*. Jo named the painting. "Hawk" is a slang name for a person who preys on others: a killer. She thought it suited the ominous mood of the picture.

Edward started the composition in 1941, right after the Japanese bombed Pearl Harbor. People in New York were scared. At night they used blackout curtains in case enemy planes attacked. "Hitler has said that he intends to destroy New York and Washington," wrote Jo in her diary. Edward captured this feeling of menace in his painting. It shows a diner on a deserted city street late at night. Garish green light inside the diner contrasts with darkness outside. Through the plate-glass window, the viewer sees three people sitting at the counter, not speaking to one another. "E. [Hopper] posed for the 2 men in a mirror," wrote Jo, "and I for the girl. He was about a month and half working on it—interested all the time, too busy to get excited over public outrages." Later Edward told an interviewer that the picture was "based partly on an all-night coffee stand [he] saw on Greenwich Avenue in downtown New York." When asked if *Nighthawks* represented loneliness, he said, "I didn't see it as particularly lonely. I simplified the scene a great deal and made the restaurant bigger. Unconsciously, probably, I was painting the loneliness of a large city."

Nighthawks, 1942

Edward Hopper, 1963

Edward rarely commented on his art. "If you could say it in words, there'd be no reason to paint," he said. He let the paintings speak for themselves. Once, when he was pressed to make a statement for a catalogue accompanying a show of his work, he said, "Great art is the outward expression of an inner life in the artist . . . his personal vision of the world."

Toward the end of Edward's life, a journalist asked him what advice he would give a young artist just starting out. Edward answered with a single word. "Work!"

Author's Note

Edward Hopper's vision of America still rings true. His pictures tell stories about a time and a place and invite endless questions.

After seeing an exhibit of Hopper's paintings, the viewer goes outside and looks at the world through the artist's eyes: The warm tones of brick buildings; architectural details such as rooftops, windows, and pillars; and the intense blue of a cloudless sky. Capturing all this in painting meant everything to Hopper. Despite serious illnesses and surgeries, he kept working until almost the end of his life. He died sitting in a chair in his studio at 3 Washington Square North on May 15, 1967, two months before his eighty-fifth birthday. In an obituary *Life* magazine said, "Hopper distilled, more masterfully than any other artist of his time, a haunting look and mood of America."

Acknowledgments

At Abrams I want to thank my editor, Howard Reeves, for working on this book with me and bringing it to life. A special thanks to Maggie Lehrman for her assistance. And a huge bouquet of appreciation to the gifted Celina Carvalho for designing the book. To Jason Wells, publicity and marketing director, I owe many thanks for his sustained and tireless efforts on my behalf.

During the course of research, many people helped me. I particularly want to thank Sarah O'Holla, Kristen Richards, and Anastasia Levadas at the Whitney Museum of American Art Library. Through them I found Elizabeth Thompson Colleary, art historian, author, and teacher, who generously provided new visual material and helped me contact the Sanborn Collection. At the Frick Art Reference Library, I also thank Lydia Dufour, chief of public services.

As always I am deeply grateful to George Nicholson for his enthusiastic interest and guidance throughout the project. And a big thank you to his assistant, Thaddeus Bower.

Expressions of appreciation would be incomplete without mentioning my writer friends, "Lunch Bunch" and the Thursday Night Group.

Most of all I thank my husband, Michael, for sharing with me a love of art.

Appendix

Edward Hopper's art school friends and their remarkable achievements:

Josephine Verstille Nivison

Jo took night classes at the New York School of Art, known as the Chase School, in 1905. At that time Edward was there, and they both studied painting and life drawing with Robert Henri. Jo, as she was called, captured Henri's attention, and he asked her to pose for a life-size portrait. She greatly admired Henri, and posing for him helped her learn more about doing portraits of her own. But her favorite subject was cats!

In 1904, Jo had earned a bachelor of arts degree from the Normal College of the City of New York, and she supported herself by teaching at an elementary school. However, her passion was art. During the summer she visited New England art colonies and produced cheerful oils and watercolors of houses, beaches, and boats.

In those days, the early part of the twentieth century, few women were able to show and sell their paintings, but Jo was determined to establish herself as an artist. She particularly liked doing watercolors, and in 1914 started to exhibit her work in many group shows. She also sold drawings to various newspapers. When she rented her own studio in New York, she held tea parties to show her artwork. After she married Edward and they spent their honeymoon painting, Jo exhibited her watercolors at The Art Institute of Chicago, and the Whitney Studio Club and the Morton Gallery in New York. Although Edward's career soon overshadowed hers, Jo struggled to maintain her own artistic identity throughout her life. Recently, more than two hundred of her paintings, mostly watercolors, have been rediscovered, and there is renewed interest in her work.

Guy Pène du Bois

Edward Hopper met Guy Pène du Bois at the Chase School when they were both young art students, and they remained lifelong friends. Du Bois was born in America but descended from a French family and appreciated Edward's love of French culture.

After art school du Bois went to Paris to continue his training. When he returned to New York, he followed in his father's footsteps and became a reporter for *The New York American*, a newspaper. Then he branched out as an art critic. As early as 1916, he showcased Edward's Parisian watercolors in a publication called *Arts and Decoration*.

In the 1920s du Bois wrote witty pieces for magazines such as *Vanity Fair* and *The New Yorker*. But in 1924 he wanted to focus on painting again and moved to France with his wife and children. They settled in the little town of Garnes, near Paris, and stayed for six years. "It was in Garnes that I learned to paint," recalled du Bois in his autobiography, *Artists Say the Silliest Things*. Paintings such as *Americans in Paris*, *Shops*, and *Morning, Paris Café* reflect his interest in the people around him, especially Americans living abroad.

When du Bois and his family came back to New York, he continued to paint scenes of city life as well as portraits of "flappers" and society hostesses. He exhibited widely and quickly gained recognition. Today his paintings can be seen in many major museums.

George Bellows

One of Edward's most famous classmates at the Chase School was George Bellows. Bellows, a dashing, athletic man, loved sports and played on the school's baseball team, which competed with their rivals at the Art Students League. Success came early to Bellows with his dynamic drawings and paintings of the boxing ring: *Club Night*, 1907, and *Stag at Sharkey's*, 1909. Edward recalled attending boxing matches with a fellow art student, and most likely it was Bellows. Their teacher, Robert Henri, considered Bellows his star pupil.

Under Henri's influence, Bellows turned to portraiture and portrayed immigrant children on New York's Lower East Side: *Frankie the Organ Boy, Paddy Flannigan,* and *Little Girl in White*. A tender portrait of his elderly father in his hometown of Columbus, Ohio, led to commissions from important society people to have their pictures painted. When Bellows married Emma Story, a classmate from the Chase School, she, and then their daughters, became his favorite subjects.

Bellows, like Edward and some of their art school friends, spent summers painting in New England. The dramatic beauty of Monhegan Island, Maine, inspired him to create powerful seascapes and landscapes. By 1911, Bellows had his first painting acquired by a museum, the Metropolitan Museum of Art in New York. During his brief career, he produced approximately seven hundred works.

On January 8, 1925, when Bellows was forty-three years old, he died suddenly from a ruptured appendix. At the funeral his teacher, Henri, wept uncontrollably. Edward expressed his grief in a somber painting, *Day after the Funeral*.

However, Bellows had assured his place in the history of twentieth-century American art.

Rockwell Kent

Rockwell Kent started out as an architecture student. During the summers, though, he studied painting with William Merritt Chase and won a scholarship to the Chase School. In the spring of 1902, Kent enrolled in Robert Henri's night class. By fall he was a full-time student with classmates Edward, George Bellows, and Guy Pène du Bois. Kent regarded Edward as the John Singer Sargeant (a revered American artist) of the class, who could be counted on to turn out "an obviously brilliant drawing."

Kent was the first of them to take Henri's advice and go to Monhegan Island to paint. The wild setting thrilled him. Unlike Edward, who later went to Monhegan just for the summer, Kent stayed on during the winter. The next summer he bought a piece of land on Monhegan Island, built his own house, became a lobsterman, and yet found time to paint. When he showed his work in New York, critics gave him rave reviews. Even George Bellows was jealous of Kent's paintings and vowed he would go to Monhegan and paint "better ones!"

Kent married, had a son, and in 1910 opened an art school on the island. His praises of Monhegan encouraged Edward to go there in 1916 and again in 1917, when he saw another old art school friend, Josephine Nivison.

Although Kent loved his family, he felt restless and longed for adventure. Throughout the years he kept taking off on journeys to Newfoundland, Alaska, Greenland, and Tierra del Fuego. During his stay in Alaska, he developed skill as a woodblock engraver and became a printmaker and illustrator. He wrote books about his travels and illustrated them himself. Back in New York, Kent designed logos for publishers such as Viking Press. In 1927 his path crossed Edward's again when they belonged to the same organization, the American Print Makers, and exhibited their work together. Kent even had an apartment and studio in Edward's building, 3 Washington Square North.

The publication that brought Kent the most fame was Herman Melville's *Moby-Dick*. For this project Kent created 270 strong pen-and-ink drawings, and designed every detail of the deluxe, limited edition published in 1930.

Robert Henri

Robert Henri, the popular teacher who mentored so many successful students, urged them to depict American scenes and American subjects. Although Henri had studied in France and valued the work of European artists, he championed the need for an American art. Born in the Nebraska territory, Henri grew up on the frontier, and his rugged spirit reflected his background.

By the time he started teaching at the New York School of Art in 1902, Henri had already established himself as a painter and was particularly known for his portraits, many featuring children. Under his influence Edward made portraits of models and friends, often depicting his classmates at their easels. Looking back he described Henri as a "good teacher" and said, "He dealt not just with the meticulous things of painting but related painting to life." In class Henri read literary works, especially those by American writers such as Ralph Waldo Emerson and Walt Whitman, to excite and inspire his students. "Paint what you feel," he said. "Paint what you see. Paint what is real to you."

And Edward took those words to heart.

Henri stayed at the New York School of Art until 1908, then taught at its rival school, the Art Students League, from 1915 to 1927. The New York School of Art, known as the Chase School, was renamed the Parsons School of Design in 1941.

References and Resources

(*) denotes materials suitable for younger readers

Books

Benson, E. M. *John Marin: The Man and His Work*. Washington: The American Federation of Arts, 1935.

Cowart, Jack, and Juan Hamilton. *Georgia O'Keeffe: Arts and Letters*. Boston:Washington, National Gallery of Art in Association with New York Graphic Society Books and Little, Brown and Company, 1987.

du Bois, Guy Pène. *Artists Say the Silliest Things*. New York: American Artists Group, Inc., and Duell, Sloan and Pearce, Inc., 1940.

Early Drawings of Edward Hopper, introductory essay by Gail Levin. New York: Kennedy Galleries, 1995.

Emmerling, Leonhard. *Jackson Pollock*. Koln: Taschen, 2003.

*Foa, Emma. *Edward Hopper*. New York: Franklin Watts, A Division of Scholastic Inc., 2003.

Goodrich, Lloyd. *Edward Hopper*. New York: Abradale Press/Harry N. Abrams, Inc., 1983.

———. *Edward Hopper*. New York: Harry N. Abrams, Inc., 1989.

John Marin: Watercolors, Oil Paintings, Etchings. New York: The Museum of Modern Art, 1966.

Kransfelder, Ivo. *Edward Hopper: Vision of Reality*. Koln: Taschen, 2006.

Levin, Gail. *Edward Hopper: A Catalogue Raisonné*. New York: The Whitney Museum of American Art in Association with W. W. Norton & Co., 1995.

———. *Edward Hopper: An Intimate Biography*. Berkeley: University of California Press, 1998.

———. *Edward Hopper*. New York: Crown Publishers, 1984.

———. *Edward Hopper: The Art and the Artist*. New York: W. W. Norton & Company in Association with the Whitney Museum of American Art, 1980.

———. *Edward Hopper As Illustrator*. New York: W. W. Norton & Co., 1979.

Quick, Michael, and Jane Meyers, Marianne Doezema, and Franklin Kelly. *The Paintings of George Bellows*. New York: Harry N. Abrams, Inc., 1992.

Schmied, Wieland. *Edward Hopper: Portraits of America*. Munich: Prestel, 2005.

Sutton, Denys. *Degas: Life and Work*. New York: Artabras, A Division of Abbeville Press, 1991.

Traxel, David. *An American Saga: The Life and Times of Rockwell Kent*. New York: Harper & Row, Publishers, 1980.

Articles

Colleary, Elizabeth Thompson. "Josephine Nivison Hopper: Some Newly Discovered Works," *Woman's ArtJournal*, Spring/Summer 2004, pp. 3–11.

Schiffenhaus, J. Anton. "A Window into the World of Edward and Josephine Hopper," Pilgrim & Provincetown Museum, 1996.

Shattuck, Kathryn. "In Hopper's Realm, Ending a Long Day or Starting a Long Night," *The New York Times*, Sunday, July 9, 2006, Art, p. 21.

Pamphlet

*Heyl, Lawrence Jr. "The Birthplace and Boyhood Home of Edward Hopper," Hopper House, Nyack, New York.

Picture Credits

Cover and page 43 top: Edward Hopper, American, 1882–1967, *Nighthawks*, 1942. Oil on canvas. 84.1 x 152.4 cm. Friends of American Art Collection, 1942.51. The Art Institute of Chicago. Photography © The Art Institute of Chicago. **Page 2:** *(Self-Portrait)*, 1925–30. Oil on canvas. 25 1/4 x 20 5/8 in. Whitney Museum of American Art, New York. Josephine N. Hopper Bequest. 70.1165. © Heirs of Josephine N. Hopper, licensed by the Whitney Museum of American Art. Photograph by Robert E. Mates. **Page 3:** Edward Hopper and his sister, Marion Hopper, n.d. Photograph. The Arthayer R. Sanborn Hopper Collection Trust—2005. © Heirs of Josephine N. Hopper, licensed by the Whitney Museum of American Art. **Page 4:** *(Elizabeth Griffiths Smith Hopper, The Artist's Mother)*, c. 1915– c. 1916. Oil on canvas. 37 1/2 x 29 in. Whitney Museum of American Art, New York; Josephine N. Hopper Bequest. 70.1191. © Heirs of Josephine N. Hopper, licensed by the Whitney Museum of American Art. Photograph by Sheldan C. Collins 10/3/06. **Page 5 top:** *(Shops and Delivery Wagon)*, c. 1892. Pencil on paper. 8 x 10 inches. Whitney Museum of American Art, New York; Josephine N. Hopper Bequest. 70.1554.16. © Heirs of Josephine N. Hopper, licensed by the Whitney Museum of American Art. Photograph by Geoffrey Clements. **Page 5 bottom:** *Garret Henry Hopper, Artist's Father*, c. 1900. Courtesy of the Frick Art Reference Library. **Page 6:** *The Catboat*, 1922. Etching. Sheet: 13 3/8 x 15 3/4. Whitney Museum of American Art, New York; Josephine N. Hopper Bequest. 70.1008. © Heirs of Josephine N. Hopper, licensed by the Whitney Museum of American Art. Photograph by Sheldan C. Collins. **Page 7:** *Alone, Alone All, All Alone*, c. 1898. Ink on paper. 4 x 5 in. **Page 7:** *Edward Hopper Boxing with Wallace Tremper*, 1900. Pen and ink on paper. **Page 8:** *Self-Portrait*, 1903. Charcoal on paper. 47 x 30.5 cm. National Portrait Gallery, Smithsonian Institution, Washington, D.C., U.S.A. Photo: National Portrait Gallery, Smithsonian Institution / Art Resource, NY. **Page 9:** Robert Henri (American, 1865–1929), *The Art Student (Miss Josephine Nivison)*, 1906. Oil on canvas. 77 1/4 x 38 1/2 in. Milwaukee Art Museum, Purchase, M1965.34. **Page 10:** Edward Hopper in Paris, 1907. Photograph. The Arthayer R. Sanborn Hopper Collection Trust—2005. © Heirs of Josephine N. Hopper, licensed by the Whitney Museum of American Art. **Page 11:** *(French Woman with Basket)*, 1906–07. Watercolor and graphite on paper. 14 13/16 x 10 1/2 in. Whitney Museum of American Art, New York; Josephine N. Hopper Bequest. 70.1331. © Heirs of Josephine N. Hopper, licensed by the Whitney Museum of American Art. Photograph by Sheldan C. Collins 10/3/06. **Page 12:** Edgar Degas, *The Rehearsal*, 1876–77. Copyright The Frick Collection, New York. **Page 13:** *New York Pavements*, 1924 or 1925. Chrysler Museum of Art, Norfolk, VA. Gift of Walter P. Chrysler, Jr., 83.591. © This image may not be reproduced without written permission. **Page 14:** *Tugboat with Black Smokestack*, 1908. Oil on canvas. 20 1/4 x 29 1/4 in. Whitney Museum of American Art, New York; Josephine N. Hopper Bequest. 70.1192. © Heirs of Josephine N. Hopper, licensed by the Whitney Museum of American Art. Photograph by Geoffrey Clements. **Page 15:** *Écluse de la Monnaie*, 1909. Oil on canvas. 23 3/4 x 28 13/16 in. Whitney Museum of American Art, New York; Josephine N. Hopper Bequest. 70.1178. © Heirs of Josephine N. Hopper, licensed by the Whitney Museum of American Art. Photograph by Geoffrey Clements. **Page 16:** *Sailing*, c. 1911. Oil on canvas. 24 x 29 in. Carnegie Museum of Art, Pittsburgh: Gift of Mr. and Mrs. James H. Beal in honor of the Sarah Scaife Gallery. 72.43. **Page 17:** *Under Control*, c. 1907–10. Gouache on illustration board. 13 x 10 in.

Page 19: *(Boy and Moon)*, 1906–07. Watercolor and ink on paper. Sheet: 21 13/16 x 14 3/4 in. Whitney Museum of American Art, New York; Josephine N. Hopper Bequest. 70.1349. © Heirs of Josephine N. Hopper, licensed by the Whitney Museum of American Art. Photograph by Geoffrey Clements. **Page 20:** *Night Shadows*, 1921. Etching. Sheet: 13 5/16 x 14 1/4 in. Whitney Museum of American Art, New York; Josephine N. Hopper Bequest. 70.1048. © Heirs of Josephine N. Hopper, licensed by the Whitney Museum of American Art. Photograph by Sheldan C. Collins. **Page 21:** *(Hopper's hat on his etching press)*, n.d. Conté crayon on paper. 11 1/8 x 15 1/4. Whitney Museum of American Art, New York; Josephine N. Hopper Bequest. 70.344. © Heirs of Josephine N. Hopper, licensed by the Whitney Museum of American Art. Photograph by Sheldan C. Collins. **Page 22 left:** *(Blackhead, Monhegan)*, 1916–19. Oil on panel. 8 9/16 x 12 in. Whitney Museum of American Art, New York; Josephine N. Hopper Bequest. 70.1668. © Heirs of Josephine N. Hopper, licensed by the Whitney Museum of American Art. Photograph by Robert E. Mates. **Page 22 right:** *Jo Painting*, 1936. Oil on canvas. 18 1/4 x 16 1/4 in. Whitney Museum of American Art, New York; Josephine N. Hopper Bequest. 70.1171. © Heirs of Josephine N. Hopper, licensed by the Whitney Museum of American Art. Photograph by Geoffrey Clements. **Page 23:** *The Mansard Roof*, 1923. Watercolor over graphite on off-white, moderately thick, moderately textured wove paper. 13 7/8 x 20 in. Brooklyn Museum. 23.100. Museum Collection Fund. **Page 24:** *Chop Suey*, 1929. Collection of Barney A. Ebsworth. **Page 25:** *(Jo Sketching at Good Harbor Beach)*, 1923–24. Watercolor on paper. 13 7/8 x 20 in. Whitney Museum of American Art, New York; Josephine N. Hopper Bequest. 70.1129. © Heirs of Josephine N. Hopper, licensed by the Whitney Museum of American Art. Photograph by Geoffrey Clements. **Page 26:** *(Victorian House)*, 1923–24. Watercolor and graphite on paper. 13 7/8 x 19 7/8 in. Whitney Museum of American Art, New York; Josephine N. Hopper Bequest. 70.1432. © Heirs of Josephine N. Hopper, licensed by the Whitney Museum of American Art. Photograph by Sheldan C. Collins 10/3/06. **Page 27:** Georgia O'Keeffe, *Radiator Building—Night, New York, 1927*. Fisk University Galleries, Nashville, Tennessee. **Page 28:** *Room in Brooklyn*, 1932. Oil on canvas. 29 1/8 x 34 in. Museum of Fine Arts, Boston. The Hayden Collection—Charles Henry Hayden Fund, 35.66. Photograph © 2007 Museum of Fine Arts, Boston. **Page 29:** *Apartment Houses*, 1923. Oil on canvas. 24 x 28 15/16 in. Courtesy of the Pennsylvania Academy of the Fine Arts, Philadelphia. John Lambert Fund. 1925.5. **Page 29:** *Room in New York*, 1932. Oil on canvas. 29 x 36 in. Sheldon Memorial Art Gallery and Sculpture Garden, University of Nebraska–Lincoln, UNL–F. M. Hall Collection. Photo © Sheldon Memorial Art Gallery. **Page 30:** *House by the Railroad*, 1925. Oil on canvas. 24 x 29 in. Given anonymously. (3.1930). The Museum of Modern Art, New York, NY, U.S.A. Digital Image © The Museum of Modern Art/Licensed by SCALA / Art Resource, NY. **Page 31 top:** *New York Movie*, 1939. Oil on canvas. 32 1/4 x 40 1/8 in. Given anonymously. (396.1941). The Museum of Modern Art, New York, NY, U.S.A. Photo Credit : Digital Image © The Museum of Modern Art/Licensed by SCALA / Art Resource, NY. **Page 31 bottom left:** *Palace: Study for New York Movie*, 1939. Conté crayon on paper. 8 7/8 x 11 7/8 in. Whitney Museum of American Art, New York; Josephine N. Hopper Bequest. 70.111. © Heirs of Josephine N. Hopper, licensed by the Whitney Museum of American Art. Photograph by Sheldan C. Collins. **Page 31 bottom right:** *Study for New York Movie*, 1939. Conté crayon on paper. 11 x 15 in. Whitney Museum of American Art, New York; Josephine N. Hopper Bequest. 70. 272. © Heirs of Josephine N. Hopper, licensed by the Whitney Museum of American Art. Photograph by Sheldan C. Collins. **Page 32:** John Marin, *Region of Brooklyn Bridge Fantasy*, 1932. Watercolor on paper. Sheet: 22 x 28 3/16 in. Image: 17 x 22 1/8 in. Whitney Museum of American Art, New York; Purchase. 49.8. Photograph by Geoffrey Clements. **Page 33:** *The Lighthouse at Two Lights*, 1929. Oil on canvas. 29 1/2 x 43 1/4 in. The Metropolitan Museum of Art, Hugo Kastor Fund, 1962 (62.95). Photograph © 1990 The Metropolitan Museum of Art. **Page 34:** *Jo in Wyoming*, 1946. Watercolor on paper. 13 15/16 x 20 in. Whitney Museum of American Art, New York; Josephine N. Hopper Bequest. 70.1159. © Heirs of Josephine N. Hopper, licensed by the Whitney Museum of American Art. Photograph by Steven Sloman. **Page 35:** *Early Sunday Morning*, 1930. Oil on canvas. Overall: 35 3/16 x 60 1/4 in. Framed: 68 1/2 x 43 in. Whitney Museum of American Art, New York; Purchase, with funds from Gertrude Vanderbilt Whitney. 31.426. Photograph by Geoffrey Clements. **Page 36:** *Hills, South Truro*, 1930. Oil on canvas. 69.5 x 109.5 cm. © The Cleveland Museum of Art, Hinman B. Hurlbut Collection 2647.1931. **Page 37:** *Portrait of Edward Hopper*. Photograph. Arnold Newman Collection. Arnold Newman. **Page 38:** *House at Dusk*, 1935. Oil on canvas. 36 1/4 x 50 in. Virginia Museum of Fine Arts, Richmond. The John Barton Payne Fund. Photo: Ron Jennings. © Virginia Museum of Fine Arts. **Back cover and page 39 left:** *Ground Swell*, 1939. Oil on canvas. 36 1/2 x 50 1/4. The Corcoran Gallery of Art, Museum Purchase, William A. Clark Fund. **Page 39 right:** Jackson Pollock, *Composition with Pouring II*, 1966. Hirshhorn Museum and Sculpture Garden, Smithsonian Institution, Gift of Joseph H. Hirshhorn, 1966. Photograph by Lee Stalsworth. **Page 40:** *Cape Cod Evening*, 1939. Oil on canvas. 30 1/4 x 40 1/4 in. National Gallery of Art, Washington. John Hay Whitney Collection. 1982.76.6. This photograph is not to be used for publication, commercial or advertising purposes without written permission from the National Gallery of Art, Photographic Services, Washington D.C. 20565 U.S.A. **Page 41:** *Gas*, 1940. Oil on canvas. 26 1/4 x 40 1/4 in. Mrs. Simon Guggenheim Fund. (577.1943). The Museum of Modern Art, New York, NY, U.S.A. Digital Image © The Museum of Modern Art/Licensed by SCALA / Art Resource, NY. **Page 42:** Josephine N. Hopper, *Self-Portrait*, [n.d.]. Watercolor on paper. Sanborn Collection. **Page 43 bottom:** *Edward Hopper*, 1963. Photograph by Hans Namuth. Courtesy Center for Creative Photography, University of Arizona. © 1991 Hans Namuth Estate.

Source Notes

Page 3: "I do not exactly . . . well enough to do." Edward Hopper quoted in Lloyd Goodrich, *Edward Hopper* (New York: Abradale Press/Harry N. Abrams, Inc., 1983), p. 152. **Page 3:** "even as a tiny lad." Marion Hopper quoted in Gail Levin, *Edward Hopper: An Intimate Biography* (Berkeley: University of California Press, 1998), p. 16. **Page 4:** "In every artist's . . . in the earlier." Edward Hopper quoted in Gail Levin, *Edward Hopper: A Catalog Raisonné* (New York: Whitney Museum of American Art in Association with W.W. Norton & Company, 1995), Volume I, p. 41. **Page 6:** "it didn't sail very well." Edward Hopper quoted in Goodrich, p. 11. **Page 8:** "Henri was . . . a magnetic teacher." Edward Hopper quoted in Gail Levin, *Edward Hopper: The Art and the Artist* (New York: W.W. Norton & Company in Association with the Whitney Museum of American Art, 1980), p. 17. **Page 10:** "[He was] the . . . at school." Guy Pène du Bois quoted in Levin, *Intimate Biography*, p. 124. **Page 10:** "Ed Hopper down . . . try illustrating." Walter Tittle quoted in ibid., p. 48. **Page 11:** "Paris is a . . . beautiful city." Edward Hopper quoted in ibid., p. 49. **Page 11:** "Every street . . . red pants." Edward Hopper quoted in ibid., p. 50. **Page 11:** "I do not believe . . . the French." Edward Hopper quoted in ibid., pp. 56–57. **Page 11:** "I am painting . . . or Charenton." Edward Hopper quoted in ibid., p. 67. **Page 11:** "were painted . . . touched afterward." Edward Hopper quoted in Goodrich, *Edward Hopper* (New York: Harry N. Abrams, Inc. 1989), p. 19. **Page 12:** "The light was . . . over the housetops." Edward Hopper to Alexander Eliot, quoted in Goodrich, *Edward Hopper* (1983), p. 13. **Page 14:** "They were too light." Edward Hopper quoted in Levin, *Intimate Biography*, p. 75. **Page 14:** "national art." Robert Henri quoted in ibid, p. 75. **Page 17:** "Something about . . . series of pictures." Guy Pène du Bois quoted in Levin, *Edward Hopper: The Art and the Artist*, p. 27. **Page 17:** "I never stopped painting." Edward Hopper quoted in Goodrich, *Edward Hopper* (1989), p. 28. **Page 17:** "boyhood boating . . . sloop rig." Edward Hopper quoted in Levin, *Intimate Biography*, p. 86. **Page 17:** "I was a rotten . . . mediocre, anyway." Edward Hopper quoted in Goodrich, *Edward Hopper* (1989), p. 31. **Page 17:** "I'd walk around . . . the lousy thing." Edward Hopper quoted in Goodrich, *Edward Hopper* (1983), p. 21. **Page 18:** "What I wanted . . . side of a house." Edward Hopper quoted in ibid., p. 21. **Page 18:** "As a child . . . the lower part." Edward Hopper quoted in Levin, *Intimate Biography*, p. 540. **Page 18:** "Maybe there is . . . comes slowly." Edward Hopper quoted in ibid., p. 88. **Page 21:** "most intense black ink." Edward Hopper quoted in Goodrich, *Edward Hopper* (1983), p. 23. **Page 21:** "I got this . . . pose for me." Edward Hopper quoted in Levin, *Intimate Biography*, p. 117. **Page 22:** "In those days . . . young artist." Edward Hopper quoted in ibid., p. 113. **Page 22:** "Returned." Edward Hopper quoted in ibid., p. 130. **Page 23:** "adored pussy cat." Josephine N. Hopper quoted in ibid., p. 163. **Page 23:** "Hey, I saw . . . yesterday." Josephine N. Hopper quoted in ibid., p. 168. **Page 23:** "At Gloucester . . . looking at houses." Edward Hopper quoted in ibid., p. 169. **Page 23:** "It interested . . . always interested me." Edward Hopper quoted in ibid., p. 169. **Page 24:** "a worm's eye . . . bird's eye view." Edward Hopper quoted in ibid., p. 169. **Page 24:** "Frog went . . . gangly frog." Josephine N. Hopper quoted in ibid., p. 170. **Page 27:** "Mademoiselle." Josephine N. Hopper quoted in ibid., p. 576. **Page 27:** "Just like my grandmother's." Edward Hopper quoted in ibid., p. 185. **Page 29:** "The idea had . . . many impressions." Edward Hopper quoted in Levin, *Edward Hopper* (Crown, 1984), p. 60. **Page 30:** "He did it . . . many of them." Josephine N. Hopper quoted in Levin, *Intimate Biography*, p. 195. **Page 30:** "She always . . . everything." Edward Hopper to Katharine Kuh quoted in ibid., p. 539. **Page 32:** "The emphasis . . . thing is overdone." Edward Hopper quoted in Goodrich, *Edward Hopper* (1983), p. 70. **Page 32:** "It is hard . . . than Edward Hopper." Lloyd Goodrich quoted in Levin, *Intimate Biography*, p. 203. **Page 32:** "the brilliant modernists." Henry McBride quoted in ibid., p. 253. **Page 34:** "He sat in . . . managed somehow." Josephine N. Hopper quoted in ibid., p. 38. **Page 34:** "her tallest handicap." Bertram Hartman quoted in ibid., p. 552. **Page 35:** "It wasn't . . . someone else." Edward Hopper quoted in Levin, *Edward Hopper: The Art and the Artist*, p. 46. **Page 35:** "We like it . . . starting another." Edward Hopper quoted in Levin, *Intimate Biography*, p. 230. **Page 36:** "was done . . . were terrible." Edward Hopper quoted in ibid., p. 231. **Page 36:** "a canvas that . . . from 6 to 8PM." Josephine N. Hopper quoted in ibid., p. 231. **Page 36:** "Things looked . . . joy of it." Josephine N. Hopper quoted in ibid., p. 232. **Page 36:** "Bird Cage Cottage." Edward and Josephine N. Hopper quoted in ibid., p. 250. **Page 37:** "Beautiful exhibition . . . accomplished artists." Edward Alden Jewell quoted in ibid., p. 252. **Page 38:** "All the birds . . . rest too." Hopper quoting from Goethe's "Wanderer's Nightsong," ibid., p. 266. **Page 39:** "It ought . . . beauty." Josephine N. Hopper quoted in ibid., p. 314. **Page 39:** "He's too . . . lose that way." Josephine N. Hopper quoted in ibid., p. 269. **Page 39:** "bad painter . . . photography is." Clement Greenberg quoted in ibid., p. 396. **Page 39:** "Art is like . . . hard work." Edward Hopper quoted in ibid., p. 539. **Page 40:** "Mental impressions . . . some evening sound." Edward Hopper quoted in ibid., p. 313. **Page 40:** "there was this . . . got his sketch." Richard Lahey quoted in ibid., p. 313. **Page 41:** "an effect of night . . . pumps lit." Josephine N. Hopper quoted in ibid., p. 328. **Page 41:** "When we got . . . studio entirely now." Josephine N. Hopper quoted in ibid., p. 328. **Page 42:** "Ed's canvas . . . in the distance." Josephine N. Hopper quoted in ibid., p. 329. **Page 42:** "Hitler has said . . . and Washington." Josephine N. Hopper quoted in ibid., p. 348. **Page 42:** "E. [Hopper] posed . . . public outrages." Josephine N. Hopper quoted in ibid., p. 349. **Page 42:** "based partly on . . . downtown New York." Interviewer for *Vogue*, June 1954, "The America of Edward Hopper," quoted in ibid., p. 349. **Page 42:** "I didn't see it . . . of a large city." Edward Hopper quoted in ibid., p. 349. **Page 43:** "If you could . . . to paint." Edward Hopper quoted in Goodrich, *Edward Hopper* (1983), p. 57. **Page 43:** "Great art is . . . of the world." Edward Hopper, *Statement Three*, quoted in ibid., p. 153. **Page 43:** "Work!" Edward Hopper to Rafael Squirru quoted in Levin, *Intimate Biography*, p. 566.

Some museums where you will find work by Edward Hopper

The United States

Metropolitan Museum of Art, New York City

Museum of Modern Art, New York City

Whitney Museum of American Art, New York City

Cleveland Museum of Art, Cleveland, Ohio

Museum of Fine Arts, Boston, Massachusetts

National Gallery of Art, Washington, D.C.

Harvard University Art Museum, Cambridge, Massachusetts

Museum of Fine Arts, Houston, Texas

Fine Arts Museum of San Francisco, California

Yale University Art Gallery, New Haven, Connecticut

Carnegie Museum of Art, Pittsburgh, Pennsylvania

The Art Institute of Chicago, Chicago, Illinois

Walker Art Center, Minneapolis, Minnesota

Virginia Museum of Fine Arts, Richmond, Virginia

England

Tate Gallery, London

Spain

Thyssen–Bornemisza Museum, Madrid

To Edwin P. and Patricia Moldof, and Stephen and Sandra Mendelsohn Rubin
—SGR

Library of Congress Cataloging-in-Publication Data:

by Rubin, Susan Goldman.
Edward Hopper / by Susan Goldman Rubin.
p. cm.
ISBN-13: 978-0-8109-9347-1 (hcj)
ISBN-10: 0-8109-9347-3
1. Hopper, Edward, 1882–1967. 2. Painters—United States—Biography. I. Title.

ND237.H75R83 2007
760.092--dc22
[B]
2006031978

Text copyright © 2007 Susan Goldman Rubin
Book design by Celina Carvalho

Published in 2007 by Abrams Books for Young Readers, an imprint of Harry N. Abrams, Inc.

Printed and bound in China
10 9 8 7 6 5 4 3 2 1

HNA ▮▮▮▮▮
harry n. abrams, inc.
a subsidiary of La Martinière Groupe

115 West 18th Street
New York, NY 10011
www.hnabooks.com